#61301
8.1/3.0

TRIANGLE HISTORIES
★★★★ ★ ★★★★
THE CIVIL WAR

FREDERICK
DOUGLASS

Helaine Becker

BLACKBIRCH PRESS, INC.
WOODBRIDGE, CONNECTICUT

Published by Blackbirch Press, Inc.
260 Amity Road
Woodbridge, CT 06525
Web site: http://www.blackbirch.com
e-mail: staff@blackbirch.com
© 2001 Blackbirch Press, Inc.

Printed in China

10 9 8 7 6 5 4 3 2 1

Photo credits:
Cover, pages 4, 6, 8, 12, 14, 17, 20, 22, 25, 41, 44, 46, 48, 56, 58, 70, 79, 88: ©North Wind Picture Archives; cover (inset), pages 10, 27, 32, 35, 38, 54, 61, 78, 82, 85, 87, 93, 97: The Library of Congress; pages 50, 66, 80, 90: The National Archives; pages 64, 76: National Portrait Gallery; page 65: Denver Public Library Western History Department; page 75: Blackbirch Press archives.

Library of Congress Cataloging-in-Publication Data
Becker, Helaine.
Frederick Douglass / by Helaine Becker.
        p. cm. — (The Civil War)
Includes bibliographical references (p.   ) and index.
        ISBN 1-56711-557-8 (hardcover: alk. paper)
1. Douglass, Frederick, 1817?–1895—Juvenile literature. 2. African American abolitionists—Biography—Juvenile literature. 3. Abolitionists—United States—Biography—Juvenile literature. 4. Antislavery movements—United States—History—19th century—Juvenile literature. [1. Douglass, Frederick, 1817?–1895. 2. Abolitionists. 3. African Americans—Biography. 4. Antislavery movements.] I. Title. II. Civil War (Blackbirch Press)
E449.D75 B43 2001
973.8'092—dc21   2001000726

CONTENTS

PREFACE: THE CIVIL WAR

Nearly 150 years after the final shots were fired, the Civil War remains one of the key events in U. S. history. The enormous loss of life alone makes it tragically unique: More Americans died in Civil War battles than in all other American wars combined. More Americans fell at the Battle of Gettysburg than during any battle in American military history. And, in one day at the Battle of Antietam, more Americans were killed and wounded than in any other day in American history.

As tragic as the loss of life was, however, it is the principles over which the war was fought that make it uniquely American. Those beliefs—equality and freedom—are the foundation of American democracy, our basic rights. It was the bitter disagreement about the exact nature of those rights that drove our nation to its bloodiest war.

The disagreements grew in part from the differing economies of the North and South. The warm climate and wide-open areas of the Southern states were ideal for an economy based on agriculture. In the first half of the 19th century, the main cash crop was cotton,

Slaves did the backbreaking work on Southern plantations.

grown on large farms called plantations. Slaves, who were brought to the United States from Africa, were forced to do the backbreaking work of planting and harvesting cotton. They also provided the other labor necessary to keep plantations running. Slaves were bought and sold like property, and had been critical to the Southern economy since the first Africans came to America in 1619.

The suffering of African Americans under slavery is one of the great tragedies in American history. And the debate over whether the United States government had the right to forbid slavery—in both Southern states and in new territories—was a dispute that overshadowed the first 80 years of our history.

For many Northerners, the question of slavery was one of morality and not economics. Because the Northern economy was based on manufacturing rather than agriculture, there was little need for slave labor. The primary economic need of Northern states was a protective tax known as a tariff that would make imported goods more expensive than goods made in the North. Tariffs forced Southerners to buy Northern goods and made them economically dependent on the North, a fact that led to deep resentment among Southerners.

Economic control did not matter to the anti-slavery Northerners known as abolitionists. Their conflict with the South was over slavery. The idea that the federal government could outlaw slavery was perfectly reasonable. After all, abolitionists contended, our nation was founded on the idea that all people are created equal. How could slavery exist in such a country?

For the Southern states that joined the Confederacy, the freedom from unfair taxation and the right to make their

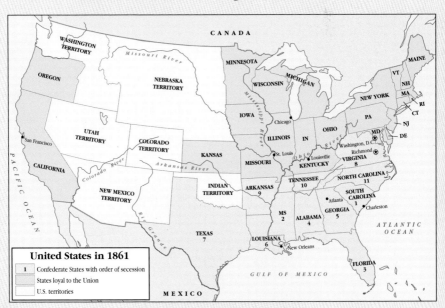

own decisions about slavery was as important a principle as equality. For most Southerners, the right of states to decide what is best for its citizens was the most important principle guaranteed in the Constitution.

The conflict over these principles generated sparks throughout the decades leading up to the Civil War. The importance of keeping an equal number of slave and free states in the Union became critical to Southern lawmakers in Congress in those years. In 1820, when Maine and Missouri sought admission to the Union, the question was settled by the Missouri Compromise: Maine was admitted as a free state, Missouri as a slave state, thus maintaining a balance in Congress. The compromise stated that all future territories north of the southern boundary of Missouri would enter the Union as free states, those south of it would be slave states.

In 1854, however, the Kansas-Nebraska Act set the stage for the Civil War. That act repealed the Missouri Compromise and by declaring that the question of slavery should be decided by residents of the territory, set off a rush of pro- and anti-slavery settlers to the new land. Violence between the two sides began almost immediately and soon "Bleeding Kansas" became a tragic chapter in our nation's story.

With Lincoln's election on an anti-slavery platform in 1860, the disagreement over the power of the federal government reached its breaking point. In early 1861, South Carolina became the first state to secede from the Union, followed by Mississippi, Florida, Alabama, Georgia, Louisiana, Virginia, Texas, North Carolina, Tennessee, and Arkansas. Those eleven states became the Confederate States of America. Confederate troops fired the first shots of the Civil War at Fort Sumter, South Carolina, on April 12, 1861. Those shots began a four-year war in which thousands of Americans—Northerners and Southerners—would give, in President Lincoln's words, "the last full measure of devotion."

OPPOSITE: The Confederate attack on Fort Sumter began the Civil War.

Introduction:
"I Resolved to Fight"
★ ★ ★ ★ ★

Frederick Douglass

Frederick Bailey had been a troublesome slave to his master. He had not only taught himself to read, he was teaching other slaves. The solution was simple: Sixteen-year-old Frederick would be sent to work for several months the farm of the dreaded "slave breaker" Edward Covey.

True to his reputation, Covey worked Frederick to exhaustion and whipped him for the slightest offense. One blistering afternoon, when Frederick sat down in a field, feeling faint, Covey came up behind the young man and clubbed him over the head with a hickory slat.

Covered with blood, Frederick ran seven miles home to his master and begged to be taken back. But the master sent him back to Covey, saying that the farmer would never kill him, it would cost too much. Frederick dragged his aching body back to the farm.

Strangely, Covey did not immediately punish the young slave for running away.

Early in the morning a few days later, however, as Frederick tended Covey's horses in the barn, he felt a rope slip around his ankles. Spinning around in fright, he saw Covey tightening the rope. Giving a yank, the white man pulled Frederick's feet out from under him. Covey leaned close to the frightened slave, his face a mask of cruelty. The whipping was about to happen.

At that moment, from somewhere deep in his being, Frederick Bailey would later write, "Cowardice departed. Bold defiance took its place." Grabbing Covey around the throat, Frederick pulled himself up as the white man pulled away. "I resolved to fight," he wrote. Covey called to a white worker nearby for help. When the man came close enough to help Covey in the fight, Frederick knocked him over with a hard kick to the ribs.

Frederick and Covey clawed, punched, and wrestled in the white man's barn for almost two hours. At last, Covey sat down, panting and bloody. He hadn't meant to beat Frederick so badly, he claimed, but the slave had resisted. Frederick smiled inwardly, knowing that he had won the fight and the only blood that had been spilled belonged to the slave breaker.

The man, who would later become famous as Frederick Douglass, would remain a slave for several more years. But in his mind, the day he fought back against the evil slave breaker was the day he truly became free.

9

Chapter 1

The man Americans know as Frederick Douglass was born into slavery as Frederick Augustus Washington Bailey in 1817 on a farm on the Eastern Shore of Maryland. His mother, Harriet Bailey, was a slave owned by Colonel Edward Lloyd, the largest slave owner in Maryland.

Today, the word slavery often brings to mind large cotton plantations in the Deep South. It was, however, the area surrounding the Chesapeake Bay—Maryland, Delaware, and Virginia—where slavery began and was a way of life for almost 200 years before big cotton plantations arose. At the time of Frederick Bailey's birth, almost two-thirds of the slaves in the United States lived in the farmland around the Chesapeake Bay, which was within 100 miles of major cities such as Baltimore, Philadelphia, and Washington, D.C.

OPPOSITE: Slaves work on a tobacco plantation.

11

Slave cabins in the 1800s had dirt floors and were barely fit for humans to live in.

Large farms arose in this area because the enormous Chesapeake Bay had many ideal ports for shipping goods abroad—and for bringing in slaves. In addition, most Native American tribes had been eliminated from the region, making it a perfect area for raising tobacco and wheat. The labor of black slaves became the foundation of this area's economic system.

Frederick was born on one of several farms owned by Lloyd. His father was widely believed to be the master of the farm, Aaron Anthony. While that belief was never proved, it is certain that Douglass' father was, in fact, a white man.

★

In 1824, when Frederick was seven, Stonewall Jackson was born, a little more than 100 miles away in Virginia.

★

Frederick hardly knew his mother. Slaves and their children were regularly separated from each other, sometimes when the children were less than a year old. This was done as an attempt to weaken family bonds. In later life, Douglass could only remember the vaguest impressions of his mother. He recalled her coming in late at night, after working in the fields, to lie down beside him. She usually walked back out to the fields while Frederick was still asleep. Harriet Bailey died when Frederick was around seven years old. No one mentioned her death to her son until some time later.

Frederick's grandmother took care of him until he was five. She was too old to work in the fields, and so her job was to look after the youngest slave children. When he was old enough, Frederick left his grandmother and went to live with the other, older children at the main plantation, including several of his brothers and sisters.

Life for a slave, even for a child, was one of constant hardship. There was never enough to eat. Corn meal mush, the daily meal, was thrown into a trough, or tray, which was set upon the ground. Children pushed and shoved to reach the

Slave cabins were cold and uncomfortable, without wooden floors or fireplaces as shown in this drawing.

food. Some used discarded oyster shells to scoop up the mush, but most ate with their bare hands. The strongest children got the most food. But even they went to bed hungry.

Worse than the hunger was the cold. Slaves slept on the dirt floor of shabby quarters, using whatever they could find as a blanket. Many years later, as a middle-aged man, Fredrick Douglass wrote of his life as the slave boy Frederick Bailey.

"I suffered much from hunger, but much more from cold. In hottest summer and coldest winter, I was kept almost naked—no shoes, no stockings, no jacket, no trousers, nothing but a coarse linen shirt, reaching only

to my knees. I had no bed. I must have perished with
cold, but that, the coldest nights, I used to steal a bag
used for carrying corn to the mill. I would crawl into this
bag, and there sleep on the cold, damp, clay floor, with
my head in and feet out. My feet have been so cracked
with the frost, that the pen with which I am writing
might be laid in the gashes."

Even though he suffered terribly, young Frederick was still better off than many older slaves. Most worked in the fields from before sunrise to after sundown, then cooked, mended, and washed to prepare for the next day. When they finally rested, they just dropped where they were and fell into a weary sleep.

Cold and fatigue were not the worst of their troubles, either. Slaves were regularly whipped or beaten. Even a sideways look could earn a slave thirty lashes. Any slave accused of breaking a rule, even a simple direction, would be punished. Few slaves escaped the lash completely, no matter how old, sick, or hardworking.

★

Jefferson Davis, who became president of the Confederacy, refused to allow his slaves to be whipped.

★

Even though slaves were valuable property to owners, punishment sometimes resulted in death. As a child, Frederick knew of murders on the farm. In one case, a slave ran into a river to avoid punishment. The overseer warned him to come out by the count of three or be shot. When the slave refused to leave the water, the overseer killed him. In another

15

incident, Frederick's cousin was beaten to death by her owner because she had fallen asleep and did not hear the owner's baby cry.

The master of the farm, Aaron Anthony, seemed to take pleasure in beating his slaves. And Frederick's Aunt Hester was a frequent target of Anthony's rage. Once, Frederick was awakened by his aunt's screams and saw Anthony whipping her. He had never witnessed such a horrible scene before. Terrified, he hid in a closet, afraid that he would be next.

That awful memory would haunt Frederick for the rest of his life. He remembered it as the time he first came to hate slavery and all it stood for.

A Debate Over Slavery

At the same time a slave child in Maryland was getting his first bitter taste of slavery, the debate over slavery reached the halls of Congress—a little more than fifty miles away—for the first time. In 1820, while Frederick was under the care of his grandmother and his mother worked dawn to dusk in the fields, the territory of Missouri asked to be admitted to the Union. Since slavery was permitted in the Missouri Territory, however, Northerners who objected to slavery had no intention of admitting it. They called on their state representatives to deny Missouri's statehood. When Missouri's

★

Confederate general Robert E. Lee's father, a Revolutionary War hero, died in 1820, when Lee was 13.

★

Slaves were often whipped by overseers—bosses who were sometimes slaves themselves.

statehood bill was brought before the House of Representatives, New York Congressman James Talmadge proposed an amendment restricting slavery within its borders.

Southern lawmakers were shocked by the proposed amendment. They had been blind to the opposition to slavery brewing in Congress. After all, other slave states had been admitted to the Union. Alabama had been admitted as a slave state only months earlier with no objection. Southern legislators had overlooked that fact that with Alabama in the Union, there were eleven free states and eleven slave states. Admitting Missouri as either free or slave would shift the balance in Congress.

17

The debates in Congress over the issue revealed for the first time how divided the two regions of the nation had become. The North, for example, saw no injustice in the proposed amendment that would restrict slavery.

Southern lawmakers, however, saw Missouri as "one of their own"—an agricultural region populated by Southerners and their slaves. To them, the Talmadge Amendment was a threat to their way of life. Meetings were held in towns across America to discuss the proposals. Northern meetings denounced the extension of slavery. Southerners invoked the Constitution, saying that it guaranteed the right to own slaves. Five Northern states passed resolutions protesting Missouri's admission as a slave state.

★

In 1820, Andrew Johnson, the man who took office after Lincoln's death, was a tailor's apprentice in North Carolina.

★

Meanwhile, Southern representatives argued that people had the right to determine for themselves what their institutions should be. They insisted that all new states coming into the Union have the same rights as the original thirteen states to choose or reject slavery.

The deadlock was ended with what came to be known as the Missouri Compromise, but which depended largely on another new state, Maine. In early 1820, the House passed a bill to award Maine statehood. When the bill was sent to the Senate, the Missouri petition for statehood was attached to it. Admitting Maine a free state, and Missouri a slave state, preserved the balance of power between free and slave states. For the moment, the problem was solved, but how this balanced approach would work in the future was unsettled. Congress embarked on a new course— to find a middle road.

After many weeks of debate, Congress passed the so-called "Missouri Compromise." Under the compromise, slavery would be allowed in Missouri but prohibited in any future states north of the line formed by Missouri's southern border.

The Missouri Compromise was a turning point in American history. It was the most important single issue Congress had been forced to deal with up until that point. It also marked the final forty years of debate over slavery, something that had been part of the American way of life for 200 years.

A World Opened by Words

The question of slavery meant little to Frederick, however, as he grew up in a world in which he was considered less than human and more like a piece of property. When he was about seven years old, Frederick was sent to Baltimore to live with the family of Hugh Auld, a relative of Edward Lloyd's by marriage. Years later, he remembered leaving the farm as the happiest day of his life. He wrote,

19

Baltimore, Maryland, was a busy seaport on the Chesapeake Bay.

I look upon my departure . . . as one of the most interesting events of my life. It is possible, and even quite probable, that but for the mere circumstance of being removed from that plantation to Baltimore, I should have today, instead of being here seated by my own table . . . been confined to the galling chains of slavery. Going to Baltimore laid the foundation, and opened the gateway, to all my subsequent prosperity.

Frederick had no regrets about leaving. He knew his life in Baltimore could not be worse than life on the farm. Furthermore, he had no family ties or happy memories to bind him to the farm. His mother was dead. His brother and sisters worked far from the farm. And because space was needed to house more slaves, his elderly grandmother had been sent to the woods to die. To him, the farm was nothing but a place of loneliness and cruelty.

★

In the 1820's, abolitionist John Brown operated a leather tannery in Ohio.

★

The little boy traveled by sailboat down the Miles River to the Chesapeake Bay, then north to Baltimore. Alone in a big city, having never been off the plantation before, Frederick was taken to his new home by one of the ship's hands.

Sophia Auld greeted Frederick with great warmth. Unlike her husband, Sophia did not come from a slave-owning family. She had no idea of the "proper" way to treat a slave. Frederick found her kind and gentle, unlike any white woman he had ever known.

Frederick had been sent to the Aulds to help care for their young son, Thomas. He took on his new task with great enthusiasm and would remember it as one of the happiest times of his life.

Soon after Frederick settled in, Mrs. Auld began to teach him the alphabet. Unlike many women of her time, Mrs. Auld could read and write. Before long, Frederick was spelling words of three or four letters.

One day, however, Mr. Auld found out about the lessons and became very upset. He demanded that she stop the lessons, saying that teaching a slave to read was illegal. He explained that learning to read harmed slaves because too much

The African American in this old drawing is breaking the law—slaves were not allowed to learn reading or writing.

knowledge made them unmanageable. Reading would hurt Frederick, Auld told his wife, because the boy might learn there was a life outside of slavery and realize he had no hope of attaining it.

Frederick, who was watching Thomas Auld during the argument, was impressed by what he overheard. He could see that Mr. Auld was angry and afraid. If reading was that important, Frederick decided, he would learn no matter what obstacles he faced

Unfortunately, Frederick's lessons with Mrs. Auld came to a sudden end. Even worse for Frederick, she followed her husband's direction to

Frederick Douglass

the letter. She kept a close eye on the young slave, making sure he never even looked at a newspaper or a book. Frederick realized he had to learn on his own.

"Freedom Looked From Every Star"

The plan Frederick adopted to learn to read was a simple one: bread for lessons. He made friends with white boys he met on the street. Most were poor, and often hungry. Even so, most knew how to read slightly better than Frederick. He traded scraps of bread he stole from the Auld's kitchens for a few minutes of instruction, turning as many of his young neighbors as he could into reading tutors.

Little by little, crumb by crumb, Frederick learned to read. His favorite book was called *The Columbian Orator*, a collection of essays and stories. The book was popular in the 1820s among many young readers. *The Columbian Orator* made a deep impression on Frederick.

One section of the book described a debate between a man and his slave, arguing about whether slavery was right or wrong. The slave's points were so good that the master's mind was changed. He now recognized that slavery was wrong. At the end of the tale, the master freed the slave.

That chapter, and other writings in the book, helped Frederick form clearly thought-out ideas about slavery. He also learned new words to express

23

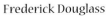

those ideas with conviction and power.

Auld's prediction that reading would make Frederick unhappy also came to pass. By the time Frederick was about twelve years old, the thought of being a slave for the rest of his life weighed heavily on him. Freedom was always in his mind. Describing those years, he later wrote that "Freedom . . . looked from every star, it smiled in every calm, breathed in every wind, and moved in every storm."

Yet freedom was still hopelessly far from Frederick's reach. At times, he was so miserable he even thought about ending his life. Instead, however, Frederick resolved to run away to the North, where there was no slavery.

A Lesson from the Shipyards

As his dream of freedom began to take shape, Frederick realized that he would need to learn handwriting rather than the printing he had mastered. Writing would enable him to forge a "pass" and possibly escape north by ship or train. To learn, he loitered at the Baltimore docks near the shipbuilding yards. Carpenters there used cursive letters as identifying marks on timbers. For example, a cursive "S" would tell the ship builders that the timber should be placed on the starboard side of a new ship.

Frederick copied the shipbuilders' marks, using bits of chalk or tar to draw them on a fence post.

A whaling ship with a leaking hull is repaired in a Baltimore shipyard. Frederick found work in the shipyards as a young man.

He added to this knowledge by having neighborhood boys teach him and by copying letters from young Thomas Auld's schoolbooks.

Before long, Frederick could match each written letter to its printed one. It took him many years of hard work, however, until he was able to write in a neat, clear, cursive hand. But it was worth the time. His skill would later become his ticket to freedom.

Frederick would have continued learning to read and write if not for events back at Anthony's farm. Anthony had died and left his property to his children, one of whom demanded that

25

Frederick return from Baltimore to work in the fields.

As Frederick sailed back to the farm, he paid close attention to which direction the boats sailed on their way to the free city of Philadelphia. His determination to run away became even stronger.

By this time, Frederick was about fourteen, and it had been nearly seven years since he had left the plantation. Almost everyone there was a stranger to him. His new owner, Master Thomas, was a cruel man, and treated his slaves much worse than any master he had ever known.

At that time, many slave owners in the Chesapeake Bay area were treating slaves with extreme cruelty. In 1831, a slave named Nat Turner and six other slaves staged a violent revolt in Virginia, at the southern end of Chesapeake Bay. Turner and his men entered the home of his master and killed the entire family as they slept. They continued on, killing any white people they came upon. Turner's force soon grew to more than forty slaves, most on horseback. By the next morning, word of the rebellion had reached whites who formed an armed militia. Soon, Turner's force scattered.

★

In 1831, across the Chesapeake Bay from Maryland, Robert E. Lee married Mary Custis, the daughter of George Washington's adopted son.

★

Before the violence ended, however, slaves had stabbed, shot, and clubbed sixty white people to death. After hiding for several weeks, Turner was finally captured, hanged, and then skinned. In all,

Frederick Douglass

Nat Turner is captured by a military officer in this old sketch.

Virginia executed fifty-five people for the revolt. In the panic that resulted from the event, close to 200 African-Americans in the Chesapeake Bay region, including many who had nothing to do with the rebellion, were murdered by white mobs. Legislatures in Virginia and neighboring states passed laws supporting the strictest policies toward all African Americans, slave or free.

Like many whites at the time, Master Thomas felt justified in his brutal treatment of slaves. He gave them so little food that Frederick was nearly always hungry. While food lay in the storehouse for Master Thomas and his family, Frederick and the other slaves were forced to beg and steal food from neighboring farms to keep from starving.

27

As Master Thomas watched the work his young slave from Baltimore did on the farm, he decided that city life had "ruined" Frederick. He didn't work hard and seemed weaker than other slaves. Even worse, Master Thomas suspected the Frederick knew how to read—and that he might be teaching other slaves. He resolved to rid Frederick of his bad habits and poor attitude by renting him out as a hired hand to a man named Edward Covey.

Covey had a frightening reputation for disciplining young slaves and breaking their spirits. Frederick went to live with Covey on January 1, 1833. Right away, Frederick was put to work as a field hand. He found the work almost impossible, having neither the knowledge of how to do the work nor the physical strength to carry it out.

The first week at Covey's farm, Frederick was almost killed when given the task of driving a cart led by oxen. Growing up in the city, he had never driven a cart or worked with oxen. The huge animals bolted and the cart was turned over, throwing Frederick to the ground. When he returned to the farm, Frederick was whipped for wasting time and ruining Covey's property.

This was only the first of many beatings that Frederick suffered at Covey's hands. The slaves were worked hard no matter what the weather, and the workdays were terribly long. "Work,

work, work," he wrote years later, "was scarcely more the order of the day than the night. The longest days were too short for [Covey], and the shortest nights too long for him."

Under this brutal treatment, Frederick sank to the lowest point of his life. Proud, stubborn, and unmanageable when he was first sent to Covey, Douglass soon became "tamed." In his autobiography, Douglass describes what happened:

> I was broken in body, soul and spirit. My natural elasticity was crushed, my intellect languished, the disposition to read departed, the cheerful spark that lingered about my eye died; the dark night of slavery closed upon me; and behold a man transformed into a brute!

★

In 1833, a general store owned by Abraham Lincoln went out of business in New Salem, Illinois.

★

To make matters worse, the Chesapeake Bay was within sight from the fields of Covey's farm. Frederick watched the ships pass by, comparing their carefree appearance to his own slavery. He called the ships "freedom's swift-winged angels." As he watched them, he prayed for delivery from bondage, and planned his escape.

Standing Up to Covey

After about six months under Mr. Covey, Frederick was weak in body and in spirit. One day, when fanning wheat, Frederick broke down.

29

The chore at hand was too difficult for one unused to such hard labor, and the sun was hot. Frederick became dizzy and his head throbbed. He paused in his work, then struggled on, afraid of the beating he would receive if he stopped. Ill with exhaustion, though, Frederick finally collapsed. He was too weak to move.

Immediately, Covey came up behind Frederick and beat him with a piece of hickory wood. Blood ran from the young man's head. He tried to get up but could not. Covey kept kicking him and shouting. Eventually, Covey left Frederick lying in the dirt.

Douglass slowly made his way back to Master Thomas's farm. Exhausted and bleeding, he begged to be released him from his work with Covey. The Master refused and sent Frederick back to the Covey farm.

Not long after his return, Covey approached Douglass with a rope. He planned to tie the slave to a post to receive a whipping. But Frederick grabbed Covey and told him that he would no longer let himself be treated like an animal. The two men fought for over two hours. At last, Covey let Frederick go.

From that moment on, Covey never beat him again. Frederick later wrote of this battle as the turning point in his life as a slave. It rekindled the embers of freedom that had been extinguished under Covey's rule.

The Evils of Alcohol

Frederick's time with Edward Covey lasted almost a year, until Christmas Day, 1833. Traditionally, the week between Christmas and New Year's Day was given to slaves as a holiday. Owners encouraged slaves to spend their "free" time in games, dancing, and drinking whiskey. It was expected that slaves would drink throughout this time.

The reason for this quickly became clear to sixteen-year-old Frederick. He saw the forced celebration as another way for masters to keep slaves under control. By allowing slaves this one week of "happiness," Frederick realized, they protected themselves from rebellion and insurrection the rest of the year. Observing this ritual for the first time as a teenager, Frederick swore he would never be tempted by alcohol.

Although he saw the evils of alcohol and slavery firsthand, Frederick was not the only person who had strong feelings about both. During the 1830s, a movement against alcohol, called the Temperance Movement, began to spread. At the same time, an even stronger movement against slavery, called abolitionism, also began to spread. A leader of both movements was William Lloyd Garrison from Massachusetts. He was a self-educated journalist who began publishing an anti-slavery newspaper, *The Liberator*, in 1831.

★

In 1834, twenty-six-year-old Andrew Johnson was elected mayor of Greeneville, Tennessee.

★

This old drawing "Slaves on the Sabbath," shows slaves enjoying themselves. In truth, few slaves celebrated.

At that time, those who spoke against slavery usually appealed to slaveholders to gradually end the practice of slavery. Garrison used the strongest language possible to call for the end of slavery "immediately," and blistered those who did not agree with him, calling them "traitors" and "hypocrites." In the first issue of *The Liberator* in 1831, he wrote:

"On this subject I do not wish to think, or speak, or write with moderation I will not retreat a single inch—AND I WILL BE HEARD."

In 1833, Garrison was one of the founders of the American Anti-Slavery Society. *The Liberator* and Garrison often aroused violent public reactions. South Carolina passed a law stating that

anyone caught handing out copies of *The Liberator* could be fined $5,000 and put in jail. In 1835, a pro-slavery mob dragged Garrison through the streets of Boston by a rope. The mayor of Boston put Garrison in jail and charged him with disturbing the peace for the incident. Strong-willed and opinionated, Garrison would cross paths with Frederick many times.

The Sabbath School

In January 1834, Master Thomas hired out Frederick to Mr. William Freeland, who was a "heavenly" master compared to Covey, Frederick recalled. He not only offered his slaves enough food to eat, but also enough time to eat it. The

slaves only worked between sunrise and sunset. They were given much work to do, but were also given good tools and enough fellow workers with which to do the assigned task.

At Freeland's farm, Frederick became acquainted with other slaves who wanted to learn how to read. They found some old spelling books, and Douglass agreed to teach them. Gradually, word spread to slaves at neighboring farms. Frederick became the leader of an illegal "Sabbath School," which met in secret every Sunday.

★

In 1835, Abraham Lincoln was elected as a state representative from New Salem, Illinois.

★

It wasn't long before the secret meetings turned to talk of freedom. With four other slaves, Frederick began to plan an escape. They would steal a canoe, paddle to the head of Chesapeake Bay, then travel on foot from Maryland to the neighboring free state of Pennsylvania, using the North Star as their guide. The date was set: the Saturday before Easter, 1835.

Douglass forged several "protection letters" for himself and his companions to show to any authorities that stopped them. The letters read,

> *This is to certify that I, the undersigned, have given the bearer, my servant, full liberty to go to Baltimore, and spend the Easter holidays. Written with mine own hand, &c., 1835.*
> *WILLIAM HAMILTON, Near St. Michael's, in Talbot County, Maryland.*

Frederick Douglass

On their day of departure, however, Frederick and his fellow slaves were discovered. Frederick managed to throw his forged pass into the fire. His companions ate the incriminating notes with their morning biscuits. Even though there was no proof, the five were led in chains to jail.

Based on Frederick's reputation, authorities considered him the probable ringleader. That meant he could not remain in Talbot County, where he would be seen as a threat to stability, and could very likely be murdered. He expected, instead, to be sold by his master and sent to a plantation in the Deep South, which had become a area of tremendous economic growth.

★

Maryland and Pennsylvania would be the sites of the two bloodiest battles in the Civil War—Antietam and Gettysburg

★

The removal of Native Americans from the Deep South to the plains opened the land for plantations.

During the first half of the 1830s, the forced removal of Native American tribes from the Deep Southern states of Georgia, Alabama, and Mississippi had opened millions of acres of land. The fertile soil and hot climate were ideal for growing cotton, and wealthy Southerners began to move inland from the Atlantic coast to build plantations on the new land.

Where wealthy Southerners went, slaves went too. In 1830, there were about 2 million slaves in the South, worth about $1 billion to their owners. Between 1830 and 1840, the slave population of Mississippi grew by 200 percent.

★

Jefferson Davis owned an 800-acre plantation near Vicksburg, Mississippi

★

Being sold "down the river" was a fate truly feared by slaves from the comparatively "soft" border state of Maryland. In the oppressive heat of Alabama or Mississippi, a slave led "a life of living death." Escape was virtually impossible.

To Frederick's surprise, however, he was not sold. Master Thomas had him released from prison. He then sent his troublesome slave back to Hugh Auld in Baltimore.

The East Baltimore Mental Improvement Society

Frederick was now eighteen years old, stood almost six feet tall, and was tremendously strong from working in the fields. His master, Hugh

Auld, knew that if Frederick learned a trade, he could be hired out for good wages—which would belong to his owner. Auld arranged for his slave to train as a caulker in the shipyards, pressing tar and other sealing material between the wood in ship's hull to prevent leaking.

Once Frederick was a skilled laborer, he was allowed to seek his own employment, as long as he turned over his weekly pay to Auld. In less than a year, Frederick was earning the highest wage possible for a slave, between eight and ten dollars a week.

In his free time, Frederick began meeting with a group of free African Americans who had formed an educational association called the East Baltimore Mental Improvement Society. At meetings, members would discuss intellectual issues. It was here that Frederick learned how to debate and sharpen his speaking skills. It was also at one of the society's meetings that he met a woman named Anna Murray. The two fell in love and became engaged.

Anna was a free woman, however, and Frederick, despite his status as a tradesman, was still a slave. His desire to marry made escaping slavery even more critical. Auld had promised Frederick that he would free him when he turned twenty-five. But Frederick did not trust Auld and did not want to wait five years or more. The only solution to his dilemma, he knew, was to escape.

37

Chapter 2

$\mathbf{A}$s Frederick became more successful at his trade, Auld allowed him to "hire out his time." Under that arrangement, Frederick agreed to pay Auld the amount Auld would earn if he had been hired out by a third party. Frederick would then be responsible for all of his weekly expenses: food, lodging, clothing, and anything else. Any money he made over and above his expenses he would be free to keep as his own. In this way, Frederick was able to save money to use for his eventual escape.

The matter came to a head when Auld revoked Frederick's hiring-out privilege because Frederick was a few days late paying his fee to Auld. In response, Frederick refused to work. When he finally decided to return to work, he lied about his wages and kept a greater share of the money he earned.

Despite appearances, however, Frederick refused to accept his situation. He resolved to escape a few weeks after returning to work. He even set the date: September 3, 1838.

OPPOSITE: An illustration of Frederick's escape, taken from the title page of a popular sheet music song about him.

39

A fugitive slave, as Frederick was well aware, was in great danger. If he was caught during the escape he could be killed or sold to slave traders. Even if his escape succeeded, Frederick knew, he would be leaving a familiar life and many friends and companions for the uncertainty of the North. Years later he wrote:

> It is impossible for me to describe my feelings as the time of my contemplated start drew near. I had a number of warmhearted friends in Baltimore—friends that I loved almost as I did my life—and the thought of being separated from them forever was painful beyond expression. Besides the pain of separation, the dread and apprehension of a failure exceeded what I had experienced at my first attempt. I felt assured that if I failed in this attempt, my case would be a hopeless one—it would seal my fate as a slave forever. It was life and death with me.

To carry out his plan, Frederick bought a train ticket to Philadelphia with money borrowed from Anna. He also obtained a sailor's red shirt, a black tie, and a "sailor's protection,"—a document certifying that the person carrying it was a free merchant seaman. The problem with the document was that it described the person who had given it to Frederick. And that description did not match Frederick's appearance. He hoped that a conductor, seeing the official look of the paper, would not study it too closely.

40

Frederick boarded a train to freedom in Baltimore.

★

In 1838, John Wilkes Booth, the assassin of Abraham Lincoln, was born outside of Baltimore, Maryland.

★

On September 3, 1838, Frederick boarded the train in Baltimore and went to the "colored" car for African Americans. His knees nearly buckled with fright when the conductor approached to check his papers. The conductor looked at the paper, then gave Frederick a quick glance. He returned the paper and continued on his way.

Several times during the trip, Frederick thought fellow passengers recognized him. Once, he was certain he saw a neighbor of the Aulds' pass by. But no one gave him away. With each passing mile, he drew closer to his dream of freedom.

The train stopped in Wilmington, Delaware, where Frederick got off and boarded a steamship bound for Philadelphia. When the ship landed, the young man who had grown up a slave set foot, for the first time, on the soil of a free state. But he was not yet safe—slave catchers roamed the streets and kidnapped African Americans. He was still in great danger.

As quickly as he could, Frederick boarded another train heading North. On September 4, after a seemingly endless journey, the train pulled into the station in New York City. Frederick was a free man.

Alone in Freedom

Frederick's arrival in New York made him a free man, but it also made him a lonely one. He knew no one in New York. He missed Anna. He had little money, no shelter, and no food.

Frederick's fear also grew worse when he learned that slave catchers continually scoured the streets of the city, focusing especially on the boarding houses that gave shelter to African Americans. He was suspicious, afraid that enemies hid behind even the kindest words. Unwilling to risk looking for a job or a place to live, Frederick wandered the streets for days, terrified of being recaptured. Finally, he approached an honest-looking African American sailor and told him of his predicament. The sailor introduced Frederick to a man named David Ruggles.

Ruggles was a prominent African American abolitionist, and a leading member of the New York Vigilance Committee—an association dedicated to helping fugitive slaves reach safety. Frederick stayed at Ruggles' house, and together the two men decided the best course of action.

Frederick told Ruggles he was a trained caulker and wanted to live where he could practice his trade. He thought Canada was likely, but Ruggles suggested New Bedford, Massachusetts, which had a free African American population and a busy port serving the whaling industry. Ruggles thought Frederick would be able to find work in the shipyards there. Best of all, slave catchers did not operate that far North, because Massachusetts was a stronghold of abolitionism.

43

Captured slaves are paraded through a town square before being returned to their masters.

Meanwhile, Douglass had written to Anna telling her of his successful escape. He asked her to join him as quickly as possible. Anna came, and Frederick and Anna were married on September 15, 1838.

A New Name and a New Life

Immediately after the wedding ceremony,
Frederick and Anna set off for New Bedford. They
began their journey on a steamship to Newport,
Rhode Island, with two bags between them and

City Hall in New Bedford, Massachusetts, a thriving seaport.

five dollars given to them as a wedding gift by Ruggles. As was usually the case traveling anywhere at that time, African Americans were separated from whites. Because the steamship did not have a great deal of space, Frederick and Anna spent their first night as newlyweds huddled on the open deck of the ship beside other African American passengers.

In New Bedford, Frederick decided, for safety's sake, to change his name. As Frederick Augustus Washington Bailey, he had never used his middle two names.

★

In 1838, Abraham Lincoln was a partner in the Springfield law firm of Lincoln and Stuart.

★

Frederick Douglass

Now he changed his last name from Bailey to Douglass, after a hero in a novel about knights in the age of chivalry. For the rest of his life, the young man from Maryland would be known as Frederick Douglass

Douglass immediately began looking for work as a caulker. He quickly discovered that, while freedom in New Bedford was better than slavery in Baltimore, it was still not a perfect life. Segregation was common, and white workers in the shipyards refused to work beside skilled African American workers.

Unable to find work in his trade, Douglass was forced to accept odd jobs shoveling coal, digging cellars, cutting wood, and loading and unloading ships. Anna worked as a house servant and as a laundress. Despite his hardships, however, Douglass enjoyed the first labor he had ever done without a master standing behind him.

As he became accustomed to his new surroundings, Douglass was shocked by the quality of life in the North. Raised in a slave society, Douglass equated slavery with wealth. He assumed that Northerners who did not own slaves were at the same economic level as poor white southerners who could not afford slaves. Instead, Douglass saw decent living conditions, even among the poorest people in New Bedford. Just as surprising were the working conditions. Douglass was amazed that workers seemed interested in their

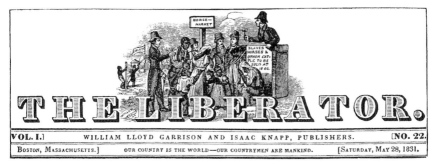

The Liberator, published by William Lloyd Garrison, was a widely read abolitionist newspaper.

tasks, and admired the way they carried themselves with a sense of pride in their abilities as tradesmen.

The most dramatic difference of all was the condition of the free African Americans. Douglass' closest friend in New Bedford, Nathan Johnson, was a day laborer. Yet, Douglass saw, his friend lived in a neater house, dined at a better table, read better books, and had a deeper understanding of current issues than any slaveholders he'd known in Maryland. Douglass also noted that former slaves who had been out of bondage for only a few years lived, on average, significantly better than the richest men in Talbot County, where he had grown up.

Seeing the good life that many had, Douglass threw himself into his work and into the care of his wife. His life became fuller when Anna gave birth to their first child, Rosetta, in June 1839. Their son, Lewis, was born in 1840.

A New Voice for Abolition

Four months after arriving in New Bedford, a young man selling subscriptions to an abolitionist newspaper approached Douglass. The newspaper, *The Liberator*, was edited by William Lloyd Garrison, the leader of the American Anti-Slavery Society. For Douglass, the paper opened the door to the powerful and growing Abolitionist movement. The articles it contained reflected his beliefs. For Garrison, there was no middle ground: slavery was evil and must be abolished. Reading his condemnation of slaveholders Douglass experienced a thrill unlike any other he had ever experienced.

Suddenly, Douglass felt he was part of a larger community that shared his opposition to "the peculiar institution." He voiced that opposition as a preacher at a local African American church. In this role, he also fought to reduce racial prejudice in the North, and opposed schemes promoted by some Southerners to force blacks to move to Africa. His article on the subject was published in the March 1839 issue of *The Liberator*.

★

Ulysses Grant entered the U.S. Military Academy at West Point, New York in 1839.

★

Douglass also became involved with the wider abolitionist movement. At meetings of the American Anti-Slavery Society, Douglass was a constant presence. He enjoyed listening to the

49

Abolitionist William Lloyd Garrison.

various speakers expose and denounce the true nature of slavery. He claimed to have no desire to speak himself, saying others could express his thoughts far better than he could.

Besides, in his heart, Douglass still felt himself to be a slave. Most of the leaders of the movement, including Douglass' hero William Lloyd Garrison, were white. Addressing an audience of white people made Douglass feel, again, the chains of bondage.

Finally, at a large anti-slavery convention held in Nantucket, Massachusetts in August 1841, Douglass could not remain silent. He spoke only briefly, but his speech impressed William Lloyd Garrison, who was in the hall. Garrison described his response to Douglass' oration in an article:

> I shall never forget his first speech at the convention—
> the extraordinary emotion it excited in my own
> mind—the powerful impression it created upon a
> crowd . . . completely taken by surprise. I think I never
> hated slavery so intensely as at that moment.

50

Garrison hired Douglass on the spot as a travelling lecturer. Along with other noted abolitionists, Douglass toured the Northern states, telling his story, selling subscriptions to *The Liberator*, and recruiting members for the American Anti-Slavery Society.

Douglass' job was to destroy pro-slavery propaganda that was flooding the North with stories of his own experiences. On the podium, he was an imposing presence. He was tall, with a powerful physique, piercing eyes and a wild mass of hair. He spoke with dramatic flair, balancing his terrible stories of the abuses of slavery with bits of humor. He made his audiences laugh—and he made them cry.

The tour was a tremendous success. One newspaper, *The Concord Herald*, praised Douglass as a speaker: "He has wit, argument, sarcasm, pathos—all that first-rate men show in their master effort." Another reported, "Flinty hearts were pierced and cold ones melted by his eloquence."

Douglass described his own popularity this way:

> "Fugitive slaves were rare then, and as a fugitive slave lecturer, I had the advantage of being the first one out. Up to that time, a . . . man was deemed a fool who confessed himself a runaway slave, not only because of the danger to which he exposed himself of being retaken, but because it was a confession of a very low origin.

51

Some of my. . . friends in New Bedford thought very badly of my wisdom in thus exposing and degrading myself."

Douglass proved so effective as a speaker that his three-month tour was extended. He spoke in New York, Massachusetts and Rhode Island, and in 1843, he went on a six-month tour of the western frontier.

His task in the West was more difficult. Feelings against slavery were not as strong there, and many whites worried that if slavery were abolished, free African Americans might move west and compete for land and jobs. For some, abolitionists were extremists and fanatics. A number of meetings at which Douglass spoke were disrupted by angry, pro-slavery mobs. Douglass and an associate were once even attacked by a group of thugs and Douglass' hand was broken.

In addition, Douglass was not treated as well as the white abolitionists with whom he traveled. He was thrown out of railroad cars when he refused to sit in the sections designated for "colored." He was forced to stay in shoddy hotels, pray in segregated churches, and accept second-class status everywhere.

Day after day, however, Douglass spoke eloquently—not only about his life on the plantation, but about the goals of the abolitionists and the racial discrimination in the North.

Many abolitionists began to fear that Douglass was becoming too effective. Many doubted audiences would believe that such a gifted speaker had actually been born into slavery. Douglass was encouraged to speak in "plantation talk" and to use less intellectual vocabulary so that his audiences would find it easier to "believe" him.

The fears of Douglass' supporters soon proved correct. An 1844 article published in *The Liberator* questioned Douglass' truthfulness. The article asked "How a man, only six years out of bondage, and who had never gone to school could speak with such eloquence—with such precision of language and thought." The prejudice of even committed abolitionists became evident to Douglass. To him, it seemed that people were saying that while slavery was wrong, African Americans should in no way be considered the intellectual equals of whites.

To defend his story, Douglass decided to write his autobiography giving the actual names of people and places from his past. Though he kept the details of his escape secret, to protect other slaves who might escape in the same manner, Douglass shared many other facts of his life, including the names of his previous masters. This was an incredibly risky decision. Federal laws at that time did not recognize Frederick Douglass as

Slave Narratives

★ ★ ★ ★ ★

During the late 1700s, a new type of literature appeared in the United States. The authors were slaves who had been freed or who had escaped and wrote under assumed names. The books were known as slave narratives. Frederick Douglass' personal narrative, published in 1845, was an immediate best seller and paved the way for many narratives that followed. Another popular slave narrative in the Midwest around that time was the autobiography of William Heyman, the first slave to publish his own poetry.

In the 1840s, Frederick Douglass became a popular speaker and a best-selling author.

a free man. Under the law, he was Frederick Bailey, property of Hugh Auld.

The Narrative of the Life of Frederick Douglass was published in the spring of 1845. William

Perhaps the most widely read slave narrative, next to Douglass', was *Incidents in the Life of a Slave Girl* by Harriet Jacobs. In 1835, at age twenty-three, after years of mistreatment, she hid in a tiny crawlspace above a cabin built by her grandmother and uncle, both freed slaves.

The space was nine feet by seven feet with a sloping ceiling three feet at the high end. Jacobs couldn't turn over while lying down without hitting her shoulder. Mice crawled over her, and there was no light or ventilation.

Her children had been bought by a friendly lawyer and were living in the same house. Harriet could watch while they played outside through a peephole she drilled. Incredibly, she lived in the crawlspace for seven years, coming out only briefly at night.

In 1842, Jacobs escaped. She sailed to Philadelphia, and traveled to New York City by train. She would later move to Rochester, New York, where she became involved with the abolitionist movement, working with Douglass. During the Civil War, Jacobs helped raise money for black refugees. After the war, she worked to improve the conditions of the recently freed slaves. She died in her late 80s.

Lloyd Garrison and fellow abolitionist Wendell Phillips both wrote introductions to the book. *The Narrative* became an overnight bestseller. It was enormously popular in the North, and also

Douglass made his audiences laugh—and cry.

sold well in Europe.

The book's popularity, however, was a double-edged sword. It gave legitimacy to Douglass' story, but it put him at tremendous personal risk. Auld could, under the law, send slave catchers to kidnap Douglass, and order them to bring the fugitive slave back to "justice" in Maryland. Douglass decided the only safe course was to leave the United States for Great Britain. Thanks to efforts by abolitionists there, all slaves in the British Empire had been freed by 1838. Douglass thought a series of lectures there might raise support among British abolitionists for the movement in America.

In 1845, leaving his wife and four children behind, Douglass toured the British Isles for nearly two years. He was a free man for the first time in his life. Even more amazing to Douglass than freedom, though, was the lack of racial prejudice.

★

In 1846, Thomas 'Stonewall' Jackson graduated from West Point.

★

Douglass' friends suggested that he settle in England, but by the fall of 1846, he was ready to return home. His true work lay in America, he said, where his fellow slaves were still in chains. In addition, he had not seen his family in almost two years.

But Douglass still risked recapture. The solution to that problem came from two of Douglass' English friends who raised the money to purchase Douglass' freedom from Hugh Auld. On December 5, 1846, the amount of $710.96 was remitted to Hugh Auld. In exchange, Auld signed the papers that released Frederick Douglass from bondage. At age 28, Douglass was at last a completely free man.

Douglass' English tour had been an huge success. Covered with glory, he returned to America in the spring of 1847 with an international reputation as a speaker and author. Now that the ransom that had been hanging over his head had been removed, he was now ready to dedicate himself to the fight against slavery, whatever the cost.

57

Chapter 3

Douglass' return to America signaled a change in his outlook and goals. He had been a loyal supporter of William Lloyd Garrison for his entire career. But now the two men disagreed about how to win the fight against slavery, and how Douglass could best serve the cause.

Garrison was a radical pacifist. His basic beliefs were formed from the passive non-resistance ideals of the Quakers. In his opinion, the United States Constitution was an immoral document because it supported slavery. Taking any political action, Garrison believed, would mean accepting the document. Instead, he thought that the way to end slavery was to persuade slaveholders of their sinfulness. Should that fail, he advocated secession of Northern states from the Union to remove itself from the "moral stain" of slavery.

OPPOSITE: An anti-slavery rally in a Massachusetts town square.

Garrison's position was extreme. He refused to vote and believed that anyone who did supported a corrupt government. For African American abolitionists, this approach was impractical. While slavery was an immoral philosophy to Garrison, for African Americans it was a daily matter of life or death.

Wealthy abolitionist Gerrit Smith held views of political action more closely aligned with Douglass'. He had already broken from Garrison's American Anti-Slavery Society to found the more politically-oriented Liberty Party. Douglass began to associate more frequently with Smith and his party.

During the 1840s, as Douglass was traveling and speaking, Smith used his extensive wealth to support programs dedicated to helping freed slaves. One program was a system of land grants. Smith donated 120,000 acres of his own property in the Adirondack Mountains of New York to freed slaves and their families so they could begin a new life in the North.

News of Smith's program spread through abolitionist communities and reached the ears of a radical abolitionist John Brown. When Brown heard about the land grants, he traveled to New York and introduced himself to Smith. There he made a proposal to Smith. Brown was an experienced farmer, and he told the wealthy abolitionist that many of the African Americans would have difficulty farming in the cold climate and rocky land of the Adirondacks. He offered to establish a family farm of his own in the area so that he could serve as an advisor to the new African American communities.

Abolitionist John Brown

Brown's offer was not only kind, it was almost beyond the understanding of Smith and many white Northerners. For a white man in the nineteenth century—even a committed abolitionist—to live and work among African Americans on an equal basis was extremely unusual. In spite of their strong beliefs that slavery was wrong, many abolitionists—like most whites of the time—viewed African Americans with prejudice and looked down on them as people. Smith liked Brown's unprejudiced idea, however, and agreed to sell Brown property for just $1 an acre. Brown then moved his family to the African American settlement of North Elba, New York, 100 miles or so south of Douglass' home of Rochester.

Douglass, who would later meet Brown, became a supporter of the newly-formed Free Soil Party, a group committed to preventing the spread of slavery west of the Mississippi River. Once Garrison's colleague, Douglass now sided with Smith and Brown.

61

★

In 1846, the United States entered a two-year war with Mexico. Among those who served were Grant, Lee, Jackson, and Jefferson Davis.

★

A difference in philosophy was not the only reason for the split between Douglass and Garrison. Douglass had also grown tired of living in the shadow of whites. He wanted to chart his own course. His dream was to publish a newspaper edited solely by African Americans, to disprove the pro-slavery argument that his people were naturally inferior to whites. Garrison objected, arguing that Douglass' greatest contribution was as a speaker. Leaving the podium would rob the abolitionist movement of one of its shining lights, Garrison said.

When Douglass decided to proceed with his plan to publish, and later to encourage his readers to engage in political action, Garrison labeled him a traitor to abolitionism. The dispute between the two became vicious, and the resulting break between them never completely healed.

The North Star

In October 1847, Douglass moved his family to the northern New York town of Rochester on the shores of Lake Ontario. Rochester had a strong abolitionist movement and was home to many active anti-slavery societies. On December 3, 1847, the first issue of Douglass' new abolitionist newspaper, *The North Star*, was published there. He named the paper after the star that guided slaves on their escape from the South.

The North Star was published weekly, and received glowing reviews. Subscriptions came in slowly, however, and expenses drained Douglass' savings. The slow start of the newspaper forced Douglass to supplement his income by returning to the lecture circuit. He traveled for six months during the first year, and was forced to borrow money using his new home as a guarantee of repayment.

But his persistence paid off. *The North Star* eventually became profitable. In 1851, Douglass was at last able to write to Gerrit Smith, "*The North Star* sustains itself, and partly sustains my large family. It has reached a living point. Hitherto, the struggle of its life has been to live. Now it more than lives." Douglass continued to publish *The North Star* in a weekly format until 1860.

★

In 1851, Stonewall Jackson began a ten-year teaching career at the Virginia Military Institute

★

Women's Rights

While *The North Star* concentrated mainly on issues of importance to African Americans, it also supported other causes, among them women's rights. Many of Rochester's feminists had been early supporters of *The North Star*. Douglass, in turn, supported the feminists and their campaign for equal rights, including the right to vote. Prominent leaders such as Elizabeth Cady Stanton, Lucretia Mott, and Susan B. Anthony considered Douglass a personal friend.

63

Lucretia Mott was a leader in the women's suffrage movement.

Douglass himself played a key role in the first women's rights convention, which was held in Seneca Falls, New York in 1848. Under attack from all sides, the delegates hesitated to make the right to vote a key demand. Unsure of what to do, Cady Stanton asked Douglass to speak to the delegates on the issue. Douglass agreed. The only man present, his bold appeal convinced the delegates that the right to vote was a key element of equality.

From that point forward, the fight for Universal Suffrage—the right to vote—was always a part of the women's rights movement. Douglass was named a lifelong honorary member of the National Women's Suffrage Association.

Battle Against Segregation

Meanwhile, Douglass continued to fight for emancipation. His position was clearly expressed in a major speech given on the Fourth of July, 1852. Douglass pointed out how Independence Day differed dramatically for whites and for African Americans. He said,

> *What to the American slave is your Fourth of July? I answer, a day that reveals to him more than all the other days of the year, the gross injustice and cruelty to which*

A family headed west during the 1840s.

he is the constant victim . . . To him, your celebration is a sham.

Douglass' powerful statement about the differing opinions of "freedom" came at a time when most white Americans believed in the "Manifest Destiny" of the United States, the belief that America was a special nation with a clear right to expand to every part of the continent. During the 1840s, more than 300,000 Americans traveled across the Great Plains to the Pacific Coast along the famous Oregon and Santa Fe Trails. During the same decade, the territory under U.S. control also grew. After a two-year war with Mexico ended in an American victory in 1848, much of the Southwest and all of California became American territories.

65

More than 300,000 Americans traveled in "prairie schooners" to land the U.S. had won in the Mexican War.

As people moved across the country to the West Coast, many settled in places along the way, including the Great Plains regions, which today are Kansas and Nebraska. And although most Americans agreed that it was their right to settle on these lands, they sharply disagreed about slavery and about government control in the new territories.

Many settlers in western territories preferred strong control by the federal government. Government land grants and railways were

Frederick Douglass

essential to life on the plains, as was government help against Native American tribes who did not want to leave their land.

James Polk, America's president during those years, was a Southern slave owner who wanted the new lands to support slavery. For slavery to survive, he knew, it would have to expand. If new free states entered the Union, slave states would eventually lose their power and influence in national affairs.

Once again, the issue became a bitter debate in Congress, as territories that had come under control after the Mexican War applied for statehood.

Neither pro- or anti-slavery forces had any hope of gaining complete victory. The only solution, as in 1820, was a compromise. Henry Clay of Kentucky, a force behind the Missouri Compromise, helped pass the Compromise of 1850. It contained several important provisions.:

★
In 1848, gold was discovered in California, and the steady stream of westward travelers became a flood.
★

- California was admitted to the Union as a free state.

- Both New Mexico and Utah were organized as territories. They would be admitted to the union as either free or slave states, based on their constitutions at the time of application.

- Slave trading was prohibited in the District of Columbia, but slavery was not abolished outright there.

67

- Severe fugitive slave laws would be enacted to protect the rights of southern slave owners.

In some ways, the Compromise of 1850 made the tensions between pro- and anti-slavery forces worse. Northern abolitionists were deeply opposed to the Fugitive Slave Laws, which said that anyone who helped an escaped slave could be prosecuted.

Throughout the early 1850s, Douglass spoke out bitterly about the Fugitive Slave Laws. Determined to end suffering wherever he could, he also actively supported anti-slavery groups such as the New York Vigilance Committee.

As active as he was in his fight against slavery, Douglass also took time to be with his wife and five children in Rochester. The Douglasses were now considered prominent members of Rochester society. While life in Rochester was good, however, it was not perfect. The public schools would not admit African Americans, and Douglass was forced to enroll his eldest daughter, Rosetta, in a private school. Even there, she was segregated from the other white children.

Frustrated, Douglass finally hired a tutor to teach his children at home. He also launched a full-fledged campaign to end racial discrimination in the Rochester school system. The battle raged on for eight years, but in 1857, Douglass was triumphant. Segregation in Rochester schools was eliminated.

Frederick Douglass

The Underground Railroad

Douglass and his newspaper acted like a beacon for fugitive slaves who came to Rochester since it was only a short distance from the Canadian border. Some mornings, when he arrived at his office, Douglass found runaway slaves camped on the front steps.

In the 1850s, the Douglass home became a major station on the Underground Railroad's route to Canada. Over the years, hundreds of men and women passed through its doors. Eventually, Douglass became the "superintendent" of the entire region's Underground Railroad system, even though Fugitive Slave Laws could have ruined his life.

John Brown and Harpers Ferry

Another committed abolitionist, John Brown, was also a station master in the Underground Railroad. In some ways, however, his hatred for slavery was more than even Douglass could understand. To many, Brown was a dangerous agitator, and to others, he was a revered hero.

Brown met Frederick Douglass in 1847 on a speaking tour of the Northeast and Western frontier. Douglass was deeply impressed by Brown. He said, "Though a white gentleman, [Brown] is in sympathy a black man, and as deeply interested in our cause, as though his own soul had been pierced with the iron of slavery."

Slaves escaping from the South.

During their discussion, Brown told Douglass that "slaves had a right to gain their liberty in any way they could," even if that meant violence. Brown described his extreme idea to someday lead an uprising of slaves against their masters. Douglass was a pacifist. After listening to Brown, however, Douglass began to believe that violence might be necessary to achieve emancipation. At abolitionist meetings, he started saying that he would be glad to see a "revolt" of the slaves. And as Congress continued to pass laws allowing slavery to spread, Douglass lost hope that the problem of slavery would be solved peacefully.

By 1857, Douglass had completely given up the idea that slavery could be ended through peaceful means. In a speech in Canandaigua, New York, Douglass made his position clear. He said slaves

70

must be prepared to gain freedom "by labor, by suffering, by sacrifice, and if needs be, by our lives and the lives of others."

By the time Douglass decided to speak about ending slavery through violence, Brown had taken action. In 1854, Senator David R. Atchison of Missouri sponsored a bill that divided the Nebraska Territory into two regions, Kansas and Nebraska. Atchison and others believed this would permit the region's eventual entry into the Union as two separate states, one "slave" and one "free." Both the Nebraska and Kansas portions of the territory sat above the southern border of Missouri. More than thirty years earlier, the Missouri Compromise banned slavery in new territories north of that line.

Northern lawmakers and abolitionists wanted the Missouri Compromise upheld, outlawing slavery in the new territories. The South, however, wanted the Missouri Compromise repealed. It recognized that unless the compromise was overturned, slave states would gradually become outnumbered because most new territory in the growing country was north of Missouri's southern boundary. Eventually, the balance of power would shift and slavery would be completely prohibited.

The debate of the Kansas-Nebraska Act was at a standstill until an amendment was added that overruled the Missouri Compromise and replaced it with the law from the Compromise of 1850. That

71

The Weeping Time

★ ★ ★ ★ ★

By 1857, Douglass had spoken out against slavery for more than twenty years. Yet the institution of slavery remained as strong as ever in the South. Ironically, though almost all Southerners supported slavery, fewer than 25 percent owned slaves. Of those who owned slaves, about 90 percent owned fewer than 20 slaves.

There were, however, many plantations served by huge groups of slaves. One of the largest was a rice plantation located in the tidewater area of southeastern Georgia. A wealthy man named Pierce Butler inherited the plantation and more than 450 slaves in 1837. During the twenty years he owned the plantation, Butler gambled and drank away most of his inheritance—more than $700,000—$10 million in today's dollars.

Because of his huge debts, Butler was forced to sell all of his possessions, including his slaves. In March 1857, about 430 men, women, and children were brought to Savannah, Georgia. Over two days, while Douglass was speaking out against slavery, the largest sale of human beings in U.S. history took place.

The sale came to be known among slaves as "The Weeping Time." One witness wrote in his diary that, "It is a dreadful affair. Families will not be separated, that is, husbands and wives, parents and young children. But brothers and sisters of mature age, parents and children of mature age, all other relations and the ties of home and long association will be violently severed."

The two-day sale brought $303,850. Pierce Butler, once again wealthy, vacationed in Europe then returned to the U.S. and settled in Philadelphia.

law stated that the question of slavery would be settled by a vote of the residents of the territory rather than by the federal government.

The Kansas-Nebraska Bill, signed into law on May 30, 1854, was a huge success for the South. The North, on the other hand, viewed the Kansas-Nebraska Act as a betrayal. Most Northerners refused to accept it. Instead, many threw their support behind a new political party, the Republican Party, which was strongly opposed to slavery.

As events unfolded, pro-slavery forces led a campaign of violence and terror in an effort to make Kansas a slave state. To fight this campaign, John Brown brought bands of Free Soil fighters to Kansas to combat the threat. During a raid on pro-slavery supporters at Pottawotamie, Kansas, Brown's band massacred five men. Shortly thereafter, an attack by pro-slavery forces left another man dead in Lawrence, Kansas. The governor declared that Kansas was in a state of open war.

Brown became a focus of national attention, and soon he returned east to continue his fight against slavery. His new plan was to stage a raid on the federal arsenal at Harpers Ferry, Virginia, steal the arms, and start a slave revolt. His effort was funded by The Secret Six, a group of wealthy New England abolitionists, including Gerrit Smith. Brown also sought Douglass' support. Douglass, however, refused, convinced that an attack on

★

In 1854, Jefferson Davis was the U.S. Secretary of War under President Franklin Pierce.

★

73

federal property would enrage most Americans and hurt the abolitionist cause.

Douglass met with Brown not far from Harpers Ferry several months before the raid. He wished Brown luck, but explained that he could not join the fight. As he left, however, Shields Green, one of his traveling companions, told Douglass that he planned to stay with "The Old Man," meaning Brown.

October 16, 1859, John Brown and his force seized the armory at Harpers Ferry. After a brief battle, two of Brown's sons were killed and Brown himself was captured. Two months later, Brown was convicted of treason and hanged. Shields Green and three other followers of Brown were hanged a short time later.

Douglass received the news of the raid while lecturing in Philadelphia. Newspaper accounts of the raid mentioned Douglass' name prominently. Letters that Douglass and Brown had exchanged before the raid were found among Brown's belongings.

Knowing that if he were arrested and charged with conspiracy, he would not be able to obtain a fair trial, Douglass fled to Canada. Once there, Douglass wrote numerous letters in his own defense. While he vigorously denied having anything to do with the raid, he nevertheless referred to Brown as a "noble old hero."

74

John Brown's "army" was captured by Federal troops at Harpers Ferry.

Douglass traveled to England for a second lecture tour that he had planned well before the raid. The story of the raid and his near arrest made his lectures even more popular with British audiences.

As Douglass was about to continue on to France, however, he received news that his youngest daughter, Annie, had died. The news devastated Douglass, and he returned home to Rochester in May, 1860.

The country to which he returned was different from the one he had left. The winds of war were blowing.

75

Chapter 4

THE CIVIL WAR YEARS

By 1860, a presidential election year, the dispute between North and South had heated to the boiling point. Many parties competed for power. The Republicans, opposed to slavery's spread into the new western territories, chose Abraham Lincoln as their candidate. The opposing Democrats were split into two groups. Moderate Northern Democrats backed Illinois Senator Stephen Douglas, while pro-slavery forces backed Vice President John Breckinridge. A newly-formed party, the Constitutional Union Party, was led by Douglass' old friend and abolitionist, Gerrit Smith.

Douglass campaigned for Smith until he realized that his friend had no real chance to win the election. At that point, Douglass switched his support to Lincoln and the Republican Party.

OPPOSITE: Abraham Lincoln became the 16th president in 1860.

77

John Breckinridge

The Democratic Party won more votes than any other party, but they were split between the two Democratic candidates. Abraham Lincoln won the election with less than 40 percent of the popular vote.

South Carolina refused to accept Lincoln's win, and in December, 1860, it became the first state to secede from the Union. Six more southern states—Georgia, Florida, Mississippi, Alabama, Louisiana and Texas—followed South Carolina's lead in February 1861. Together, they established an independent government under the name "The Confederate States of America."

Lincoln's priority was to save the Union. To do so, he tried to appease the South by promising to uphold the Fugitive Slave Laws. He also said he would allow slavery to continue in the states where it was already established.

But his efforts to save the Union were too late, the divide had become too deep. On April 12, 1861, Confederate artillery bombarded Fort Sumter. The Civil War had begun.

The War Heats Up

Lincoln sent 75,000 troops to South Carolina to put down the Confederate uprising. Immediately thereafter, four more states joined the

78

The Confederate artillery attack on Fort Sumter was observed from rooftops in Charleston, South Carolina.

The Bull Run River in Manassas, Virginia, became the site of the first major battle of the Civil War.

Confederacy: Virginia, Tennessee, North Carolina and Arkansas. Battle lines were drawn. The North, with twenty-three states and a population of 22 million, faced off against the South, with eleven states, and only 9 million people. More than a third of the South's population was slaves.

For the Confederacy, the war was about the right to secede, economic freedom, and the right to own slaves. For Lincoln and the North, the battle was about preserving the Union. For Douglass and the abolitionists, the war was about ending slavery altogether.

Douglass, who had supported Lincoln's election, was disappointed by the president's offer to the South. For him, the war presented two major goals. The first goal was the total abolition of slavery in the South and border states. The second goal was to win the right for African Americans to enlist in the Union army. He traveled the North extensively, lecturing and drumming up support for these goals.

At first, many in the North blamed the abolitionists for destroying the Union. Angry mobs had even made them targets of violence. As the war progressed, however, many of those same people came to share the abolitionist position. Douglass' persuasive speeches and writings about freeing slaves were a major factor in changing Northern views on the issue.

As the demand for emancipation grew louder, Lincoln responded by signing a bill outlawing slavery in Washington D.C. in April 1862. While Douglass considered this a step in the right direction, he did not think Lincoln had gone far enough. Lincoln, however, was concerned that the border states of Delaware, Maryland, and Kentucky would switch allegiance from the North to the South.

In the South, fierce battles raged throughout 1862. As the war dragged on without resolution, the cost to the North rose. The South, despite its smaller army, continued to win battles and push Northern troops out of the South. Union soldiers were dying on the battlefield in tremendous numbers.

81

In 1863, African American recruits were permitted to sign up for the Union Army.

The Emancipation Proclamation

Lincoln realized that he needed to take stronger action against the Confederacy. In September 1862, the North won a costly victory at Antietam, Maryland, the bloodiest day in U.S. history. Immediately after the victory, Lincoln issued the Emancipation Proclamation, which freed slaves in all states not under Union control. The Proclamation read, in part:

> *And by virtue of the power and for the purpose aforesaid, I do order and declare that all persons held as slaves within said designated states and parts of states are and henceforward shall be free . . . and I further declare and make known that such persons of suitable condition will be received into the armed service of the United States.*

82

Douglass waited eagerly for the news of the Emancipation Proclamation at a telegraph office in Boston. He later wrote, "We were waiting and listening as for a bolt from the sky. . . for the dawn of a new day. . . for the answer to the agonizing prayer of centuries." With Lincoln's proclamation, Douglass had at last achieved his goals: the abolition of slavery in the South and the acceptance of African Americans in the military.

While the Emancipation Proclamation was an important document, it was not a complete victory for Douglass and the abolitionists. It did not free the slaves in the Union border states. The Emancipation Proclamation did, however, award freedom to millions of Southern slaves. A mass exodus of slaves toward Union-controlled land followed. Many immediately fled from their homes, taking to "freedom's road."

Douglass and the Union Army

With the end of slavery in sight, Douglass turned his attention to the armed forces. The Emancipation Proclamation had given African Americans the right to fight in the Union Army. Douglass lobbied vigorously for Congress to pass laws authorizing African Americans to enlist. In 1863, Congress finally changed enlistment laws. Douglass now became an active recruiter for the Union forces.

83

The Governor of Massachusetts asked for Douglass' help in forming the first African American regiment of the Union Army, the Massachusetts 54th. Douglass responded by writing a powerful editorial, which ran in the Massachusetts newspapers. "Men of Color, to Arms!" he wrote. He encouraged African Americans to demonstrate their equality and show their patriotism by joining. Douglass' sons, Lewis and Charles, were among the first to enlist. Frederick Jr. joined them later that year.

Conditions for the African Americans in the Union Army were terrible. They were paid half of what white soldiers received and were not allowed to become officers. They were frequently given inferior weapons and inadequate training.

When Douglass learned of these conditions, he published his complaints and requested a meeting with President Lincoln to air his concerns. Douglass met with Lincoln in the summer of 1863. While he did not receive all the answers he wanted, Douglass was somewhat encouraged by Lincoln's attention to his criticism.

By the end of the war, African American soldiers made up about 10 percent of the Union army. They distinguished themselves in battle and earned a reputation as fierce fighters. By the end of war, 38,000 African American soldiers had given their lives for the victorious Union cause.

"Here Comes My Friend Douglass"

As the Civil War came to a close, Douglass became more concerned with the fate of African Americans who were newly free. His own experience had shown that freedom did not mean equality. Discrimination in the army and among civilians was still widespread. Insuring fair treatment for all African Americans became Douglass' next priority.

An African American soldier poses in his dress uniform.

In the 1864 presidential election, Democrats chose a popular general, George McClellan, as their candidate. Anti-slavery forces and abolitionists supported another general, John C. Fremont, a radical Republican and former Free Soil party candidate. Afraid that McClellan might actually win, Douglass, Fremont and the other radical Republicans eventually threw their support behind Lincoln.

Lincoln was concerned that the North might not be able to completely win the war. He feared that Confederate forces could split into guerrilla

★

On May 2, 1863, Stonewall Jackson was accidentally shot by his own men. He died ten days later.

★

In 1864, Lincoln, seeking support in border states, chose Andrew Johnson of Tennessee as his vice-presidential running mate.

bands and continue the fight for years. He worried that he might have to sign a peace treaty that left slavery intact.

Seeking advice, Lincoln invited Douglass to a second meeting. He asked Douglass to draw up an evacuation plan that would lead enslaved African Americans out of the South if the North could not win the war. At their meeting, respect between the two men grew. Douglass now considered Lincoln a friend to African Americans. And at his second inauguration, Lincoln greeted Douglass, referring to him publicly as "my friend, Douglass."

Douglass' evacuation plan was never used. In the summer of 1864, Union General William T. Sherman began his "March to the Sea." His soldiers captured Atlanta and burned the city to the ground. As the troops continued on to Savannah, they left a sixty-mile wide path of destruction and desolation. In April 1865, the Union Army captured the Confederate capital, Richmond. A few days later, Robert E. Lee surrendered at Appomattox.

On April 9, 1865, the curtain began to fall on the Civil War.

April 14, 1865

For the North, General Lee's surrender was a cause for celebration. But for the South, it was a bitter defeat, one that left their young men dead, their economy destroyed, and their land in ruins. For actor John Wilkes Booth, a Confederate supporter, the defeat was devastating. Booth had a deep resentment of Abraham Lincoln, holding him responsible for the destruction of his beloved South. With the support of the Confederate government, he had hatched a plot to kidnap Lincoln. Throughout the summer and fall of 1864, Booth attempted to kidnap the president several times, but was foiled at each turn. His final kidnapping attempt, in February 1865, failed when Lincoln changed his plans and didn't attend a crucial theatre performance.

Union General
William T. Sherman

On April 11, two days after Lee's surrender, Booth listened to a speech by Lincoln at the White House, during which the president announced that all former slaves would now become United States citizens. Booth was enraged. His kidnapping scheme was finished. The new plan was murder. On April 14, Booth shot Lincoln during a performance at Ford's Theater. Lincoln died the next morning.

The Nation Mourns

Lincoln had not been universally admired during his life. His death, however, brought an

87

outpouring of sorrow and respect from the
nation. Two days after his assassination, a parade
of mourners a mile long lined up before the
White House to pay their respects.

For Douglass, Lincoln's death was a terrible
blow. Yet despite Lincoln's death, an incredible
achievement remained: the slaves were free!
Nothing—not even the death of a president—
could take away Douglass' joy in this
long-awaited event. Douglass now needed to
insure that this victory would not be whittled
away. He campaigned tirelessly for the 13th

John Wilkes Booth shot Lincoln during a play at Ford's Theater.

Amendment to the U.S. Constitution, which would officially abolish slavery in all areas of the United States. The Thirteenth Amendment was ratified by Congress in December 1865. The Civil War, and the war against slavery, was finished.

In a meeting of the American Anti-Slavery Society in 1865, William Lloyd Garrison had proclaimed that the Society should now be disbanded, having met its goal of freeing the slaves. Douglass disagreed. It was a new era. He was determined to mark its arrival by winning the right to vote.

Chapter 5

THE RIGHT TO VOTE

In many parts of the South after the war, ex-slaves were free in name only. They still worked in servitude to their former masters and lived in poverty. Southern state legislatures passed discriminatory laws that were called the Black Codes.

The Black Codes stated that any ex-slave who did not have a steady job could be arrested and ordered to pay stiff fines. Prisoners who could not pay the fines were hired out and forced to work them off. Black children could be forced to serve as unpaid apprentices in local industries. The Black Codes also prevented African Americans from buying land, and denied them fair wages for their labor.

OPPOSITE: Andrew Johnson became the 17th president after Lincoln's assassination.

Douglass had been considering buying a farm and settling down, but when he saw that the war against slavery was ended in name only, he returned to his former role. He believed that the best way to protect ex-slaves in the South, and free African-Americans in the North, was to obtain political power through the vote.

Douglass was not alone in his beliefs. Republicans worried that Democrats might regain power in the South. If that happened, the Republicans would lose their own power as Southern states were reintegrated into the Union. The Republicans, led by two anti-slavery senators, Thaddeus Stevens and Charles Sumner, joined Douglass and the abolitionists in the campaign for voting rights. They believed that African American men would, if given the vote, support the Republican Party.

Douglass and Andrew Johnson

In the second half of 1865, Douglass traveled constantly through the North speaking out in favor of African American voting rights. He warned that the fragile peace between North and South would be endangered if former slave owners regained control of the South.

In February 1866, Douglass, his son Lewis, and three other African American leaders were invited to meet with President Andrew Johnson. The meeting was not a success. Johnson did most of the talking, and what he said was contrary to

92

A racist cartoon insulted African Americans and the Freedmen's Bureau.

Douglass' hopes. He said he intended to block voting rights for African Americans and maintain his support of southern whites' interests.

Despite their discouraging meeting, Douglass continued to gather support for his views from the North. The public was growing angry at Johnson for his refusal to punish the South and his loyalty to state's rights.

Johnson, however, did not hold all the power. Congress was controlled by the Republicans, and they wanted to break the power of former slaveholders in the South. To achieve this aim, they endorsed drastic changes. Senator Stevens demanded that the old estates be broken up and

93

The Freedmen's Bureau

★ ★ ★ ★ ★

Six weeks before his assassination, President Lincoln established the Freedmen's Bureau. This government agency was created to help war refugees get their farms working again. It also helped freed slaves—called freedmen, whether they were men, women, or children—start a new life.

The Freedmen's Bureau played an important role in the South after the war. Agency workers handed out millions of free meals to refugees, and the Bureau built hospitals and treated sick African Americans. It helped freedmen find jobs and protected them against the Black Codes.

One of the most important tasks of the Freedmen's Bureau was building schools. Teachers were sent to the South to give ex-slaves the education that had been denied to them under slavery. Under the Bureau, four colleges were set up in the South and more than 250,000 children went to school for the first time.

The Freedmen's Bureau Bill, passed by Congress in 1866, continued the funding for this popular agency. Most lawmakers felt Andrew Johnson would sign the bill. However, the bill also gave the bureau power to decided legal matters regarding civil rights. Johnson believed that local courts were the proper places to decide those questions and vetoed the bill. His veto was overturned.

distributed among the former laborers—
the ex-slaves.

The conflict between Johnson and
Congress came to a head in the summer of
1866 when two bills were passed over the
president's unsuccessful veto. The first was
the Freedman's Bureau Bill, extending the
powers of a government agency, established
during Lincoln's term. The Freedman's Bureau
provided medical, educational and financial help
to former slaves. The second bill was the Civil
Rights Bill, which gave full citizenship to African
Americans and extended all rights to them
enjoyed by white citizens.

The Fourteenth Amendment

The next step for Douglass was to establish for
African Americans the right to citizenship in the
Constitution. In the summer of 1866, Republicans
held a rally in Philadelphia to vote on a resolution
calling for African American suffrage. Douglass
attended the convention, serving as a delegate from
New York. His speech, and a speech by the woman
suffragist Anna Dickinson, helped sway the close
ballot in favor of suffrage.

Despite strong opposition from Democrats and
some Republicans, the Fourteenth Amendment was
passed in June 1866. It insured that the rights
guaranteed to blacks in the Civil Rights Bill were
now a permanent part of U.S. law.

The Fourteenth Amendment

The Thirteenth Amendment to the Constitution ended slavery, a major cause of the Civil War. With the Fourteenth Amendment, Northern lawmakers set out the terms for Southern States to rejoin the Union. Some historians consider it the most important amendment to the Constitution since the Bill of Rights.

The first section of the amendment defines citizen of the United States as anyone born or naturalized in the country. It then gives all citizens rights that cannot be taken without "due process of law," as well as guaranteeing all citizens "equal protection under the law." This section gave African Americans the benefits and protections given to any American citizen.

The second section declares that a state's representation in Congress can be reduced if it denies the right to vote to any adult male citizens.

The third section forbid any state or federal official who had left office to serve the Confederacy from holding office, unless Congress pardoned that officeholder.

The fourth section ruled that no Confederate state could pay any debts it owed.

The Fourteenth Amendment laid the cards on the table for Confederate states. Ratify it and join the Union. Reject and take your chances. Tennessee was the first Confederate state to ratify the amendment and rejoin the Union in 1866. By 1868, all states had ratified the amendment.

President Johnson reached out to Douglass, and offered him a position running the Freedman's Bureau. Douglass refused the offer, realizing that if he supported Johnson, it would give Johnson credibility as a friend to African Americans. Instead, Douglass continued to fight alongside the Radical Republicans, helping to push their goals through.

Suffragist Anna Dickinson

It was during this time that Congress passed the Reconstruction Acts requiring Southern states to conform to strict guidelines before they would be readmitted to the Union. For example, each state would have to ratify the Fourteenth Amendment and guarantee African American men the right to vote.

Johnson opposed the Reconstruction Acts. As far as Congress was concerned, this was the last straw. In 1867, Congress launched impeachment proceedings against Johnson, the first time in American history that a president faced impeachment. Although the impeachment effort was not successful—falling short by only one vote—it still managed to nullify any remaining power that Johnson held.

The Fourteenth Amendment was finally ratified by all the states in 1868. Although the amendment explicitly stated that no one could deny any person his full rights as a citizen, it did not explicitly mention the right to vote.

The Fifteenth Amendment

In the election of 1868, Douglass came out strongly against the Democratic Party, warning its members not to ignore African Americans. He also warned about the danger of new white hate groups, such as the Ku Klux Klan, which had begun threatening African Americans. Douglass greatly feared the terrorist tactics of these groups. In a speech, Douglass exclaimed, "Rebellion has been subdued, slavery abolished, and peace proclaimed, and yet our work is not done."

Douglass supported the former commander of the Union Army, Ulysses S. Grant, for president. Other African American voters also came out strongly for the Republican candidate. Partly because of their votes, Grant handily won the election. The next task on Douglass' agenda was to take the Fourteenth Amendment one step further, explicitly giving African Americans voting rights.

On March 30, 1879, the Fifteenth Amendment, giving blacks the right to vote, was passed. Douglass was elated. At the final meeting of the American Anti-Slavery Society, Douglass said, "I seem to be living in a new world."

Later Years

Douglass' later years did not bring the quiet retirement he thought he had earned. He remained active in politics, and was delighted to see large numbers of African Americans elected to state and federal offices. Douglass, however, suffered several personal and professional setbacks. A fire in 1872 destroyed his Rochester home and most of the issues of his newspapers that had been stored there. A Washington newspaper that Douglass had been asked to run failed in 1874. That same year, Douglass suffered a devastating financial loss when the Freedman's Savings and Trust Company, of which he had been put in charge, collapsed.

Douglass continued on the lecture circuit, and maintained his position as the leading spokesman for African Americans. In 1877, he was finally recognized with a political post, the largely ceremonial position of Marshal for Washington D.C.

Following his appointment, Douglass, who was now sixty, purchased an estate called Cedar Hill, near Washington. He spent a great deal of time there, welcoming his children and other visitors beneath portraits of his friends and associates. One day, he traveled from Cedar Hill to St. Michael's, Maryland, the home of his old master, Thomas Auld. Auld greeted his former slave as Marshal Douglass, and apologized for how he had behaved as a slaveholder. The two men talked for a long time and parted on good terms.

On February 20, 1895, at the age of 77, Douglass suffered a heart attack and died. African American schools closed for the day. Crowds gathered at the church where his body lay in state. Parents took their young children in for a last look at the famed leader, recognizing that no one had struggled more fiercely for them.

Douglass' Influence

Frederick Douglass had a fundamental influence on the United States of America. His vision helped to alter the interpretation of the Constitution from a document of equal rights for some into a guarantee of equality for all.

His speeches and writing helped bring about the end of slavery. His further efforts brought three important amendments—the Thirteenth, Fourteenth, and Fifteenth Amendments—into the Constitution.

Modern America's continued striving for "liberty and justice for all," has been shaped in no small part by the determination of Frederick Douglass. The slave who "resolved to fight" followed that resolution throughout his life. In doing so, he exemplified the finest tradition of the American spirit.

Glossary

abolitionism A political movement in the 1800s that sought to ban slavery. Abolitionists worked for abolition.

bondage Slavery

caulker Someone who seals a ship with tar to prevent it from leaking

compromise A settlement reached by mutual agreement of two opposing sides on an issue

debate A discussion of opposing opinions regarding an issue

emancipation Freedom

fanatics People who are overly devoted to a person or a belief

feminist Someone who believes in equal rights for women

freedmen A term used for all freed slaves—men, women, and children—after the Civil War

fugitive Someone who runs away

guerilla A soldier who engages in irregular hit-and-run warfare rather than direct battles

narrative A story

overseer A person in direct charge of slaves in the fields, a foreman

plantation A large farm in the South worked by slaves in the years before the Civil War

prejudice A negative opinion toward individuals or people of a different race, religion, social class, or other group

radical extreme

segregation Separation by race

suffrage The right to vote

temperance Moderation or avoidance of alcohol

territory A region of land that is not a state, but that has its own government

101

For More Information

Books

Banta, Melissa, *Frederick Douglass: Voice of Liberty* (Junior Black Americans of Achievement Series). New York: Chelsea House, 1993.

Coil, Suzanne. *Slavery and Abolitionists* (Liberty and Justice for All series). New York: TFC Books 1995.

Dillon Leo & Dillon, Diane. *Many Thousand Gone: African Americans from Slavery to Freedom*. New York: Knopf Books for Young Readers, 1992.

Kerby, Mona. *Frederick Douglass* (First Books Series). New York: Franklin Watts, 1995

Lyons, Mary. *Letters from a Slave Girl: The Story of Harriet Jacobs*. New York: Atheneum, 1992.

Mettger, Zak. *Till Victory is Won: Black Soldiers in the Civil War*. New York: Dutton Books, 1994.

Mettger, Zak. *Reconstruction: American After the Civil War*. New York: Dutton Books, 1994.

Patterson, Lillie. *Frederick Douglass: Freedom Fighter* (Discovery Biography Series). New York: Chelsea House, 1991.

Web Sites

American Visionaries: Frederick Douglass
http://www.cr.nps.gov/csd/exhibits/douglass/
This National Park Service site features items owned by Frederick Douglass, images of him during his long life, and highlights his achievements.

Africans in American: Abolitionism
http://www.pbs.org/wgbh/aia/part4/4narr2.html
A Public Broadcasting site that contains a narrative history of the abolition movement in the U.S. as well as links to important people, places and events of the abolition movement.

Boston African American National Historic Site
http://www.nps.gov/boaf/home.htm
This extensive site from the National Park Service contains links
to timelines of the abolition movement in Massachusetts, a
biography of William Lloyd Garrison, the Underground Railroad,
African Americans in the Civil War, and the role of the African
American church in the abolitionist movement.

Index